ALL YEAR R

Summer

Graham Sellors

Based on the Central television programmes

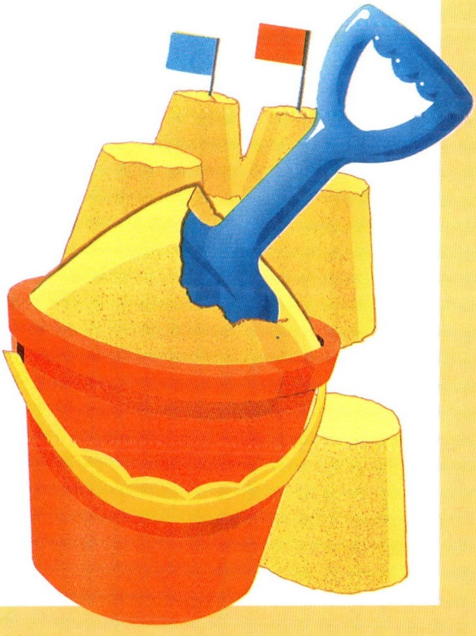

Macdonald Educational

HOW TO USE THIS BOOK

First, look at the contents page opposite. The chapter list tells you what each page is about.

If you want to know about one particular thing, look it up in the index on page 30. For example, if you want to know about air the index tells you that there is something about it on pages 12, 13 and 18. The index also lists the pictures in the book.

When you read this book, you will find some unusual words. The glossary on pages 28–29 explains what they mean.

Editor
Claire Llewellyn

Series design
Liz Black

Book design
Sylvia Tate

Production
Marguerite Fenn

Picture research
Diana Morris

Factual adviser
M G Ayres

Teacher panel
Mary Gribbin
Frances Scott

Illustrations
Clare Barber: 11
Lynn Breeze: 13, 22–3
Peter Bull: 12
John Farman: 14, 21
Toni Goffe: 6–7, 8–9
Robert Morton: 18–19
Cynthia Pow: 15, 16, 17, 24–5
Kate Rogers: 20 (left), 27
Larry Ronstadt: front cover
Sylvia Tate: 7, 20 (right)

Photographs
Barnaby's Picture Library: 13
Sally & Richard Greenhill: 8, 21
Mumtaz Karimjee: 10 (right)
NHPA: 26 (left)
Photo-Coop/Corry Bevington: 10 (left)
David Richardson: 15
Zefa: 26 (right)

CONTENTS

PLAYING

Outside and in

In summer daylight lasts longer and the weather is warmer. It's a good time for playing outside. How many outdoor games can you see in the picture below? Would you put different games in a winter picture?

Find the children playing a chasing game. Some children call this 'touch' but it has different names in different parts of the country. In some places it's called 'dobby'. What do you call it?

Some children are playing in groups, some in pairs and some by themselves. What outdoor games can you play on your own?

What's your favourite indoor game? Why do you play it inside rather than outside?

Why not make up your own games? Use your imagination to invent games with things around you. Try using newspaper, plastic bottles, cereal boxes, kitchen roll tubes, marbles and plasticine.

You could make puppets like these and act out a play or rhyme with friends.

P L A Y I N G

Now and then

Do you play computer games like 'Pacman'? Games like this work by electricity. Many modern toys and games need electricity or batteries to make them work.

Many computer games are played on television screens.

About fifty years ago, when your grandparents were young, there were no computer games and very few electrical or battery toys. They did have some toys that moved. These were clockwork and had to be wound up.

Your grandparents might have played games like the ones in the picture. Do you know any of them?

Which of these games do you still play? Are there any you have never played?

Have a good look at the picture. Can you find a whip and top, yo-yo and diabolo? They didn't need batteries or electricity to make them work. What did they need?

The children skipping would have been singing a rhyme. Do you know any skipping rhymes? Ask your grandparents or other older people about their rhymes and the games they used to play. You could use what you find out to make a 'Book of Games'.

PLAYING

Here and there

People everywhere have always played games. Yo-yos and diabolos were first used in China. So were kites. At first they were used for carrying messages, taking fishing lines out to sea and to help in fighting wars. Later, when they were used for enjoyment, many kites were made into beautiful shapes of birds and fish.

Have you ever watched a kite flying on a breezy summer's day? Does the poem remind you of it?

Cat and mouse is a game from the Caribbean.

Carrom is a game that many Indian people like to play.

The kite

How bright on the blue
Is a kite when it's new!

With a dive and a dip
It snaps its tail

Then soars like a ship
With only a sail

As over tides
Of wind it rides,

Climbs to the crest
Of a gust and pulls,

Then seems to rest
As wind falls.

When string goes slack
You wind it back

And run until
A new breeze blows

And its wings fill
And up it goes!

How bright on the blue
Is a kite when it's new!

But a raggeder thing
You never will see

When it flaps on a string
In the top of a tree.

Harry Behn

Playing with air

Kites and parachutes float on air. Some shapes float on air better than others.

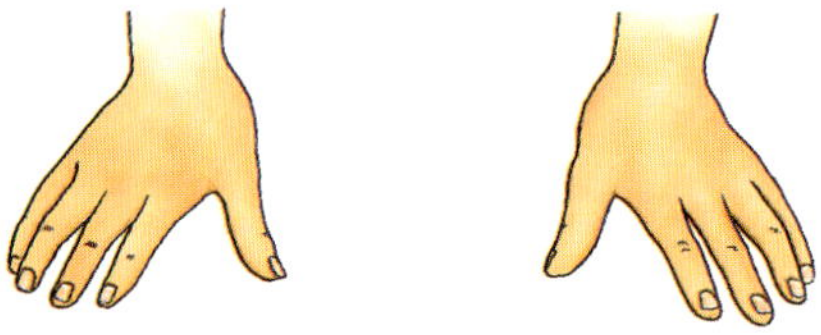

Take two pieces of paper and screw one into a ball. Hold them at the same height and let go. Which shape takes longer to fall? Why?

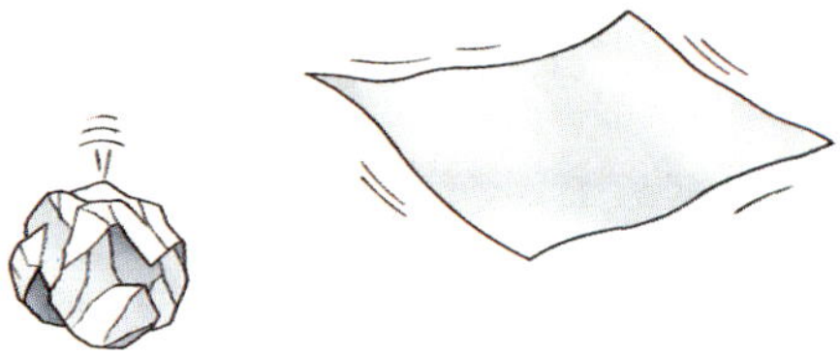

Let both pieces of paper fall at the same time.

Paper planes glide through the air. Test different shapes to see which glide furthest. To make it a fair test use the same size and kind of paper each time. Have the same person throwing and make all launches from the same place, on the same day and at the same time.

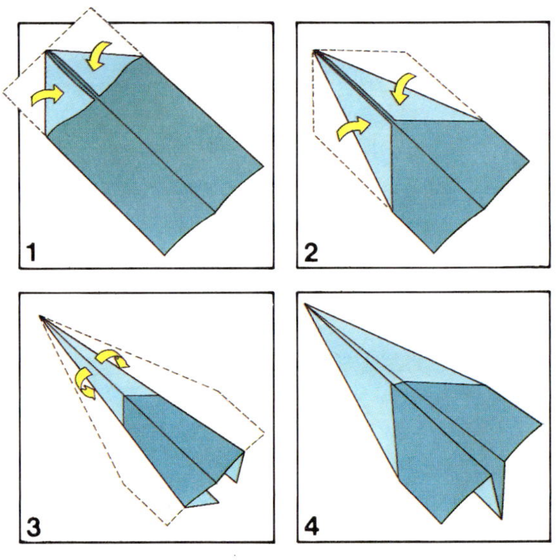

Try making planes from tissue and cardboard.

Bubbles, balloons, space hoppers and inflatables can be filled with air. This changes their shape and makes them bouncy.

What shape was this before it was blown up?

Air is free and there's plenty of it! When it moves it becomes a breeze or wind, and that can be fun for both children and adults.

Sea breezes help people sail and windsurf. They help kites fly and keep windmills turning.

MOVING

How we move

Think of all the different ways that you can move. Sometimes you move about from place to place, like when you walk or run. Sometimes you just move part of your body, like when you nod. Are any parts of you moving when you are sitting still or sleeping?

Make a list of the ways you can move your whole body and just parts of it.

Bend your finger forward and curl it round. Notice how it bends in three places. These places are where your three finger bones are joined together, and are called joints. There are lots of joints in your body. Without them, you would not be able to move.

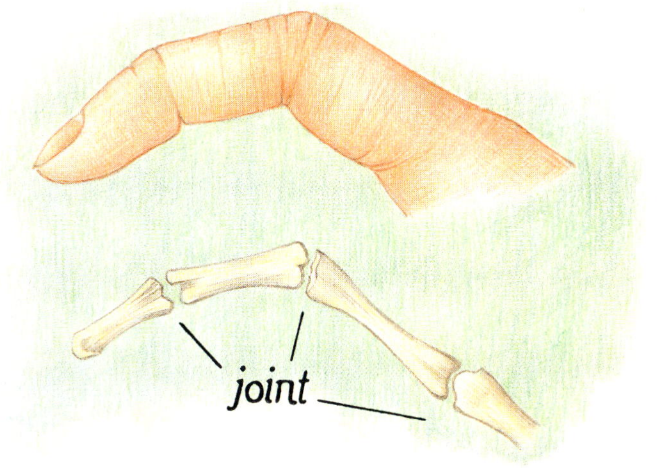

These finger joints are called knuckles.

Elbows and knees are joints. They help us bend our arms and legs. Wrists and ankles help us move our hands and feet. Some joints help us twist round. Which ones are they?

Try running without bending your elbows or knees.

MOVING

Bones and muscles

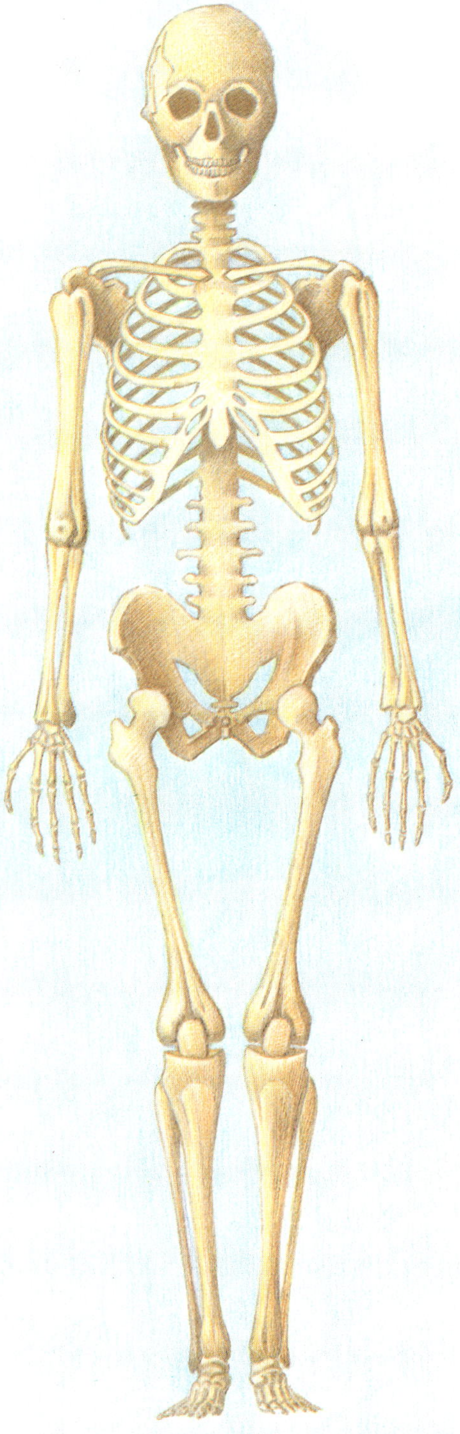

There are over 200 bones in your skeleton. They are all joined to one another so that you can move. To make this easier, your body produces a special liquid which oils your joints.

Your skeleton also protects important parts of your body. Your ribs protect your heart and lungs. What does your skull protect?

Your skeleton is a frame that holds your body up and makes you the shape you are.

Try to imagine what you would look like if you didn't have a skeleton.

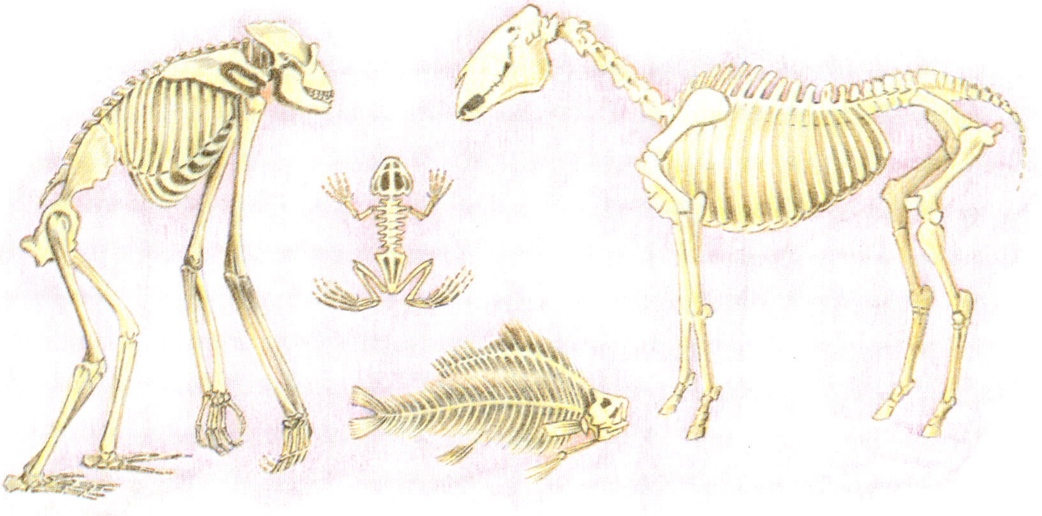

Skeletons give animals their shapes. Which animals have skeletons like these?

Bones are fastened to muscles which help them to move.

When you bend your arm, your brain sends a message to your muscles. The muscles at the front of your arm become shorter and fatter, or contract, and pull the bone in your lower arm towards them. This makes your arm bend at the elbow.

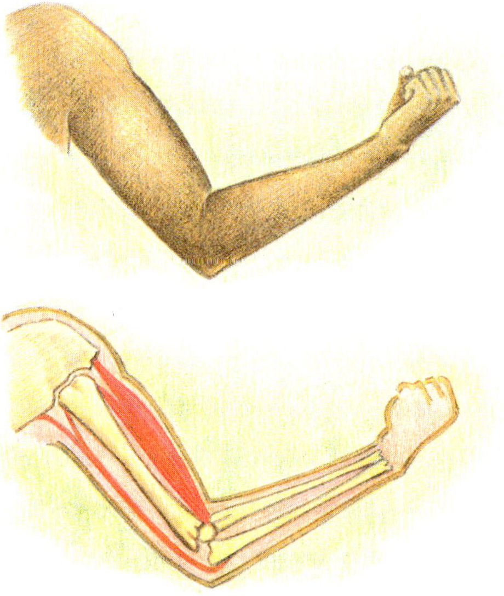

Can you feel your muscles moving when you bend your arm?

MOVING

Animals and plants

Animals move about in lots of different ways, on land, in the air, in water and underground. Birds can move on land and in the air. To help them fly they have light hollow bones and strong muscles fastened to their wings.

Fish can't move very well on land but their streamlined shape is perfect for swimming through water.

Look for creatures that swim, hop, run, fly, slither, crawl, hover, swim and run, or swim and fly.

Most animals can move about from place to place but plants are rooted to one place and can only move parts of themselves.

Plants move when they grow. Their shoots move upwards and their roots down. This movement is so slow that you can't see it. Plants also move towards light. Sunflowers turn their heads so that they face the sun.

A daisy closes at night and opens in the day.

MOVING

Making things move

What would it be like if you couldn't move? Would you be able to feed, play, write or read? Moving about is so important that people have invented machines like bicycles, cars and planes to help us move further and faster.

You can invent ways of making things move. Collect the objects in the square below and use them to help you make a matchbox move.

How many ways can you move the box on your own with nothing to help you?

No one has yet managed to invent a machine that will keep moving for ever, without ever stopping.

A toy robot can't keep moving all the time. It runs on batteries which produce electricity. After a while the batteries run down. The robot slows down and stops. Then it can't move again until some new batteries are fitted.

What other toys run on batteries?

It helps to stretch out when your body needs a rest.

You can't keep moving all the time either. After you've been moving about for a while your muscles become tired and start to ache. Have you noticed how your legs ache when you've run a long way? When this happens you have to rest until your muscles have recovered and you can begin again.

BEGINNING AGAIN

Day, week, month and year

Every day, morning, afternoon and evening come round in the same order, and at the same time. There's a pattern to each day, ending with night and beginning again next morning. This pattern is the cycle of the day.

There's usually a pattern to what you do each day too. You have your own daily cycle. In your cycle there will be some time for working, eating, playing and sleeping.

Is your daily cycle like this? Look at it carefully. Some of the sections are blank. What would you put in them if it was your cycle? Should anything else be added?

This is the cycle for a day in summer. How can you tell? What would you change if you were drawing a cycle for a winter's day?

This cycle shows a school day. Choose either a Saturday, Sunday or holiday and work out your cycle for that day.

Different people have different daily cycles. Some people go to work at night. How would their cycle be different? What about a baby that sleeps during the day and needs to be fed often?

You can work out your own cycle for a day, week, month or year. Try a yearly one. Use a calendar to help you with the dates of events that happen at the same time each year, such as birthdays or festivals like Diwali, Ramadan or Christmas.

BEGINNING AGAIN

Plant cycles

Each year has the same pattern of seasons.

There's a cycle to the way plants grow during the year. Many flowers grow, bloom, produce seeds and die all in the same year. Other plants, like trees, live for many years but they too have a yearly cycle. Each year they grow during spring and summer then, in autumn, they shed their leaves ready to survive the winter. This same pattern is repeated year after year.

Look at a horse chestnut's yearly cycle. Notice what it looks like in each season.

Conkers aren't just fun to play with, they're an important part of the horse chestnut's life cycle.

In spring the tree flowers. The flowers develop into spiky green fruits with seeds inside. These seeds are conkers. The fruits and seeds ripen during summer until they fall to the ground in autumn. Some conkers lie there through winter protected by their hard shells. In spring some of these may start to grow into new trees.

Conkers that germinate carry on the life cycle.

BEGINNING AGAIN

New life

When tadpoles hatch out they feed themselves.

At first baby mammals rely on their mothers for food.

Horses are mammals. So are sheep, pigs, mice, humans and many other animals. Mammals have babies which grow inside the mother's body until they are ready to be born. Then the mother feeds them with her own milk. Other animals like birds, insects, reptiles and fish lay eggs from which their young hatch out.

All animals try to make sure that their young survive. Some lay so many eggs that although a lot will die, some will live on. How do humans try to see that their young survive?

Some adult mayflies live for less than a day, while in America there are pine trees over 4000 years old! But nothing can live for ever. All living things must die, but they can produce more living things like themselves so that the life cycle continues.

All the plants and animals in the picture can produce young ones like themselves but not exactly the same. The baby will be like her parents but there's no one else exactly like her. And here's something wonderful! There is no one in the world exactly like you.

GLOSSARY

clockwork	Something, like a clock or toy, which is made to work by winding up a spring inside it.
contract	When your muscles contract, they become shorter and thicker.
cycle	Things which happen again and again in a regular pattern, like the seasons of the year.
diabolo	A game in which a top, shaped like an hour glass, is balanced and spun on a string stretched between two sticks.
germinate	When seeds germinate, they start to grow.
hover	Birds and insects hover when they stay in one place in the air.
imagination	When you use your imagination, you make pictures in your mind of something that is not there.

inflatable	An inflatable is something which can bc blown up by having air pumped into it.
invent	If you invent a new game, you make up a game that no one has thought of before.
launch	When you launch something, you start it off. You launch a paper planc by throwing it into the air.
reptiles	Cold-blooded animals that have lungs to breathe, and crawl or move on or near the ground.
robot	A machine that can do some of the things that humans can do.
streamlined	A streamlined shape is a smooth shape which will move easily through air or water. Fish, boats, planes and racing cars are streamlined.
survive	Things survive when they stay alivc.

INDEX

The **dark** numbers show you where there is a picture of the subject.